MW01225414

Spring is in the Air
Mandala Coloring Book

by Patricia Azeltine

www.pkburian.com

ISBN 13: 978-1546402275
ISBN 10: 1546402276

Introduction

Spring is in the Air with these Spring related mandalas. Color them in the soft colors of spring or the bright vibrant colors of summer. However, these mandalas can be colored year-round. Use your gel pens, markers, colored pencils, or ink pens. These 25 mandalas will bring you hours of relaxing fun!

Thank you for purchasing this fun book of Spring is in the Air. If you enjoyed this, a second edition is coming soon. Check my website at: www.pkburian.com. Join my newsletter to find out when the newest books come out, or go to my website to receive free pages.

Proof

Made in the USA
Columbia, SC
16 May 2017